AF413283

Roses

Roses

Collection of Little Poems

David H. Rosen

RESOURCE *Publications* · Eugene, Oregon

ROSES
Collection of Little Poems

Resource Publications
An Imprint of Wipf and Stock Publishers
199 W. 8th Ave., Suite 3
Eugene, OR 97401

www.wipfandstock.com

PAPERBACK ISBN: 979-8-3852-0109-9
HARDCOVER ISBN: 979-8-3852-0110-5
EBOOK ISBN: 979-8-3852-0111-2

VERSION NUMBER 081423

Roses blooming
work of an
earth angel

Sad but true
can't sleep . . .
tears flow

Seventy-five
happily married,but
falling apart

Oregon sunshine
smile on
my face

White roses
in memory of
a lost loved one

Inspired
by Soseki . . .
"I am a dog."

Empty pond . . .
where is the rain
to help with pain?

Retreat Center
for creative quietude . . .
thanks John Muir

Concord grapes
in the sun
the scent of youth

Yellow roses
recalling
Texas

A near collision
in the middle of the road
wild turkeys

Cool wind
sweeping away the storm
Valentine's Day

Too hot for robins,
but plenty of blue jays
in the sun

Pink and red roses
climbing in
the garden

Such serenity . . . seventy-seven

Rock roses . . .
Panda faces
in the blooms

Empty pond,
where is the rain
to help my pain?

Sixty when
I met an earth angel
in New Zealand

Retired
three times . . .
tired

Full moon
mandala morphing
in my heart

Walk through
the garden
picked a peach

Every day
is a good day . . .
no, a Tao day

I fell . . .
but remembered
how to crawl

At our house
always
February 14th

So much

depends on a red wheelbarrow

for me, a blue walker

      after William Carlos Williams

It's over
on second thought
it's just begun

At dinner
looking hungry . . .
no more

New moon
new day &
new self

Prosaic
evolves to Self
poetry

Eggplant is a case in point

Cool autumn
leaves fall &
change color

Nearly fell
but caught myself . . .
damn MS

Oregon wild roses
natives . . .
like us